Business Survival Made Simple

by Bill Edwards

About The Author

Bill Edwards is a professional writer, author, speaker, business consultant and life skills expert in his fifties. Bill has appeared on many national and international radio shows, television and web broadcasts, and been featured in a number of well-known newspapers, periodicals and publications.

Introduction

Business done right is a rare thing these days. That's why tens of thousands of small businesses, and large firms, fail every year. Whether the problem is with the boss, the employees or both, it is a terrible waste of time and effort that can be avoided with a commitment to excellence and procedural integrity. This book is for business owners, investors, managers and employees.

I hope that you will take the time to ready through this book, take notes, underline information and learn... Everything you will read about are real world situations that work for real people whether you own, invest in or work for a brick and mortar or online business. The point of this book is to teach you how to do business right. Learn and be successful.

-Bill Edwards, Make Life Work For You, http://jsi4.tripod.com

Chapter One: How Brick and Mortar Retail Stores Can Survive in an Online World of Shoppers

Nationwide chains like Best Buy and local mom and pop retail stores are facing a common and unfortunate business reality. People are coming into their stores to view and try out new items, then leaving to order the same product online from competitors offering better prices. While this may be a new problem, it might have an old solution.

Back in the early 1980s stores like Walmart, Kmart and Consumers Distributing began to take a huge bit out of the retail market. Walmart and Kmart did it by undercutting the prices charged by competitors, while Consumers Distributing offered a number of discount priced, popular products which people could order by mail, buy over the phone or instantly purchase at about five hundred catalog stores located throughout the USA and Canada.

The fact that Consumers Distributing combined catalog sales with brick and mortar locations in the J.C. Penny and Sears model was not new. Their hook was that they didn't sell everything, just the most popular items that consumers wanted. Those items were sold at terrific discounts in catalog show rooms designed with the goal of getting customers in and out fast. Their downfall was that the show room model they developed for speedy customer service never actually worked in many locations and some of the most popular or highly discounted items available in the catalog were habitually out of stock in their stores.

The novelty of the C.D. business model and their low prices kept them alive for many years with customers willing to wait to get a good deal, but customers eventually got tired of the notoriously long lines, slow service and finding so many products out of stock in their catalog show rooms. Consumers Distributing ceased to exist in 1996, but they left a legacy that we can learn from and update.

Instead of offering everything, large and small retail stores should consider scaling back to new and hot products that really fly off the shelves. On-line ordering offered in-store is another essential. Allow the option for customers to sit down at a designated computer station, browse your web site and place orders that can be filled through shipping or in-store pick up. Less stuff means less staff and overhead. That should allow real world retail locations to lower their prices and help them to compete more successfully with on-line web sites offering discounts and brick and mortar mega-sellers like Walmart.

The key is stock, speed and service. Have what you offer online in stock and get customers in and out of your doors fast. Too many stores have purchasing stations and systems that are geared to their own accounting and inventory needs, not to moving customers rapidly through the purchasing and check out process. You can also build customer loyalty by creatively bundling products together, offering exclusive deals or items and in-store amenities.

There is little doubt that virtual shopping might eventually mean the near death of most brick and mortar retail locations, but until that day comes there are still ways to successfully compete. The upside to real world retail is that consumer satisfaction with online shopping is not anywhere near what it ought to be. Everything is fine until something goes wrong, an item is damaged in shipping or you need to return it. People get frustrated by having to email customer service a thousand times or spend an hour or two on the phone choosing any one of a hundred options before they get to talk to a real person.

Real world stores can prosper through customer connectivity and product creativity. They can survive and thrive by offering on-line ordering in store, making sure all the products they sell are in stock and ready to go, having a user friendly web site and keeping it constantly updated, and making customer service job one. The day of the tired and annoyed salesperson or snotty cashier are over. Anyone that wants to get and keep a job in real world retail has to think of themselves as a partner in the business where they work.

Real world stores can add to their appeal by offering everything from snack stations and free refreshments to supervised child play rooms or areas and free product demonstration classes or seminars. Customer service experts should always be available to instantly answer questions or handle and solve any problems that pop up. Gift wrapping, local delivery and other customer amenities can also help to boost sales, cement consumer loyalty and bring in new customers through word of mouth.

Part of serving the customer well and profiting from creativity is linking up with other local businesses by offering them the opportunity to market their services or non-competing products in your store for a fee or commission. The more reasons you give a consumer to enter your store, the better chance you will have to sell something and keep the lights on while making a profit and growing your business.

Chapter Two: Are Clueless People Killing Your Business?

In the last few years we've heard that small businesses are failing in record numbers. Large corporations that were once practically guaranteed to show growth every year are reporting that sales are flat. Companies of all sizes seem to be in trouble. Why? What's going on? Is it the economy? Is it corporate reshuffling? Is it a lackluster selection of products? Is it older companies that just haven't kept up with modern consumer trends? The answer may surprise you!

As a teenager looking for work in the early 1970s, I found my job prospects limited to the typical fast food and service jobs that most high school and college students have to endure. Those jobs were just as annoying and low paying then, as now, but there was a difference. With rare exceptions, most of the people I worked made an honest effort to perform their duties correctly. Looking back, I'm actually surprised at how hard we all worked and how much pride we took in a job well done. The same could be said of most adults I knew in those days as well.

The 1980s saw a marked change in employee behavior. On the job theft and a lack of productivity among workers on all levels suddenly became real concerns for employers. Lie detector tests and even background checks were added as necessary steps in the hiring process for many jobs. It became a ritual for customers who visited any one of the major fast food chain restaurants to check their bags. Drive Thru and over the counter order mistakes then, and now, have simply become a part of the fast food consumer experience. What happened to cause these changes? The answer is obvious, or is it?

There are job candidates out there today who have been brainwashed into believing that any potential employer is the enemy. These people have every intention of doing as little work as possible, while getting as much from their employer as they can. Such problem job seekers are the kind of applicants that give potential employers the cold sweats. That's because they are harder to spot then you might think. Many are graduates from terrific schools with all sorts of fabulous recommendation letters, but is such a glowing resume really telling a prospective employer everything they need to know?

It's been my experience that a person's work ethic is revealed by any job they do. Someone who goofs off and does a half-hearted job while working at Burger King will do the same in every other paid position they ever get. It's a matter of character and personal pride. Unfortunately, future employers are unlikely to find out about any character flaws that may affect a prospective employee's future job performance. Thanks to privacy laws, it's almost impossible for them to get any kind of an employee assessment. People who have performed in a less then stellar way at any job will probably just leave that one off their resume.

If poor character is part of the problem, public education must also take some of the blame for those who lack even the most basic of skills needed for good job performance. I have met more then my share of younger people working in the service industry who couldn't count, read well or speak in a manner that would allow them to do their jobs correctly. The problem has become so great that some states now offer competency tests for first time job seekers in or just out of high school. Those who pass the tests are given a certification that they possess the basic language, math and reading skills needed to perform simple jobs or be further trained by employers.

Apart from problem job seekers, many employers are allowing clueless people to run their business into the ground. The service industry has become a textbook case study of this problem. They are allowing people with limited communication, math and language skills to represent their company. If you ask them about it, they'll just spout off some public relations spin about giving everyone a chance to succeed. In reality, they have simply dropped the ball when it comes to effective supervision and management.

We all know businesses that offer consistently bad service. While we don't say it, most consumers will avoid fast food restaurants which have short lines at lunchtime. That's because any order we place will probably be screwed up and the food we do get may not be palatable. The same can be said of hotels where checking in or out is an ordeal, retail stores without enough cashiers or too many incompetent ones and mailing stores where sending a package requires an all day commitment of time.

Employers that accept poor job performance from their employees often believe that something is better then nothing. With a critical shortage of those willing to work minimum wage or low paying jobs, many employers have just thrown up their hands and taken what they can get. Fear of losing even one employee without much hope of finding an easy replacement, often means accepting a lower level of performance from their employees. For companies with that policy, doing some business is obviously better then doing good business.

American businesses have responded to a limited pool of applicants for lower paying and minimum wage jobs by lowering their standards. Instead of hiring competent managers who can properly train, supervisor and handle their employees, many companies have decided to accept whatever level of competency and job performance their employees choose to give them. In response to those kinds of policies, floor managers and supervisors feel abandoned and stressed out. When things go wrong, they get the brunt of customer anger brought about by a general lack of effective policies that define and demand satisfactory employee behavior.

The lowering of standards has brought about an failed policy. The idea that workers need to be enticed to do a good job, rather then be expected to. Many start up Internet and technology firms have tried to entice workers to ne more productive by offering all sorts of perks. They offer child care services, work at home programs and on the job health clinics. Some companies have even went a step further by making employees their partners. Despite all these mega perks, many Internet and technology firms are in as much or more trouble then the rest of the business world. Why?

Most companies that have tried to create a utopian work environment for their employees have run into some trouble. It seems that all these efforts have managed to increase employee productivity, but only among employees who were self-starters. Those workers who were already experts at goofing off have managed to use these new tools at their disposal to perfect the art of on-the-job laziness. Why? Because a lack of effective supervision and management means employees who have no real motivation to produce.

The lowering of standards has lead many companies to accept a certain level of employee incompetence. Sadly, these companies have made the mistake of believing that their customers will also accept that lowering of standards without abandoning them. However, slip shot service will catch up to any company as the major airlines, fast food chains, retail stores and major hotels have discovered. Many of them are losing money because of overworked, underpaid or badly trained employees.

Chapter Three: Are You A Source Of Frustration or Inspiration in the Workplace?

We all know them. People who can't do it and just don't seem to get it. Something as simple as handling email, logging on and off a computer or even using a messaging system are tasks that they can never seem to master. Instead, they do things their way and seem blissfully ignorant of the frustration that they bring to the workplace.

People like that remind me of some of the characters that inevitably ended up in one or more of my classes during High School. They were the screw-ups, clowns or egomaniacs that provided an occasional distraction during a long class day. The guy who always came late. The girl that didn't know that the bathroom was the correct place for hair styling. The smelly guy who forgot to bath. The comedian that told jokes to get attention. The debater who always argued with the teacher. They were all different, but the one thing that they all had in common was an ability to bring things to a grinding halt.

Most of us are kind enough to extend some wiggle room to incompetent or eccentric people. Especially if they manage to fill some need on the job. But are we really doing them a favor? At some point the clueless, careless or incompetent person becomes a frustration that can turn any workplace into a sluggish and frustrating nightmare.

My first real job was working in a hospital kitchen. As the new guy, I was stuck at the pot sink. I had to wash out huge pots, pans and scrub off big metal cooking trays. I quickly learned that there was a right and wrong way to do things, even at the pot sink. The right way meant plenty of clean pots and pans for the cooks and an easier job for me. The wrong way meant working twice as hard, getting all wet and making the cooks angry.

There is a difference between thinking out of the box and swimming against the current. Most people agree that no system at work is likely to be perfect, but those using it can find their own shortcuts and make it work for them. People that ignore the system altogether get nowhere fast and take everyone else along for the ride.

If capitulation is the tool of the competent, justification is the tool of the clueless. People who make no real attempt to fit into the system at their at workplace always have excuses and never take responsibility for their actions. They just can't be bothered and marvel at how others get angry when their refusal to assimilate costs their coworkers time, effort or even money.

Most people who find themselves unable to fit in are using the same thoughts to fail that they could be using to succeed. It's all about removing the excuses and any support structure that is holding you back. Let's take technology for example. If you're having a problem with computers or office systems, you are not the only one. That is why hardware and software people are constantly being called to update, repair or modify systems.

Instead of trying to sidestep technology, try making friends with it. I recall how astonished people were back in the late 1980s when I bought my first portable cellular car phone. And little wonder. It took the salesperson almost an hour just to program the thing. Then there was the size. The unit weighed almost ten pounds between the battery and phone. But I was living in New York City and every time I didn't have to stand in a long line for a pay phone it was well worth it. I couldn't believe the amount of time I was saving each day and how much more I was able to get done.

Computers and office systems are designed to do the same thing. They are there to save time and increase productivity. It's estimated that for every ten seconds spent writing an email, a person saves five to ten minutes of phone time. That adds up quickly and eliminates the "I didn't get that memo (or message)" excuse. While you may never get to the point of carrying around a blackberry or checking your emails using a cell phone, you will be able to function in a world where email and some knowledge of computers had become essential.

For others, some mental housekeeping may be in order. Being unable to fit in or function as others around you do usually means that you're stuck in a rut. If that's the case, your only way out is change. Being unable to change or make adjustments that will allow you to meet the minimum expectations of a workplace is unacceptable. It's also selfish. Your inability to do your job correctly has as snowball effect. People around you are forced to adjust their routine to accommodate you.

Learning to overcome mental obstacles can open up a whole new world to those who find themselves in a rut. The key is turning the desire you have to stay where you are into a desire to move forward. It's YOU taking charge of YOU and not accepting excuses or objections that will hold you back. It's realizing that failing to fit in will cost you more time, effort and money than moving your life forward. In the process you will go from being a workplace frustration to a productive inspiration for everyone around you.

Chapter Four: Business: Surviving a Business Project

In a perfect world, any business team assembled to take on a project would be a competent group of professionals who seamlessly act as one entity. In the real world, it's a bit different. A good team tends to be made up of strong, creative, energetic and insightful members. That's the perfect recipe for egos, personalities and methods to clash. People tend to act in their own best interests and play the blame game regardless of the outcome. Here are some ideas that will help you and your team keep their eyes on the prize:

1. Keep A Log

Keeping a daily log will help you maintain contact with sources that prove valuable, learn from mistakes and develop a winning methodology. When it comes to the good, take note of that great idea, suggestion, shortcut or contact that helped bring it all home. When it comes to the bad, take note of any major problems, missed deadlines, bad numbers and the parties most responsible for those negatives. You may also want to write down your feelings as you progress through each task. This will provide emotional hindsight and give you some insight into how intuitive you may be. Being intuitive is less about possessing some sort of psychic ability and more about having a talent for being able to predict the probable outcome of a situation based on what you see happening at any given time. Intuition can be extremely helpful to a team when choosing a direction becomes convoluted by group disagreements.

2. Don't Revisit Every Decision

We live in a day when junk psychology and television psychiatrists have us going in reverse, mentally speaking. Instead of carefully considering their next move, people tend to waste time revisiting every decision they have ever made or reliving every experience or emotion they have ever had. A good project plan eliminates the need for second-guessing.

3. Make An Honest List of Your Strengths

It's wise for individual members to give serious thought to the part they can best play in the group plan before the first team meeting. When that first meeting does occur, you should be ready to cite instances where your talents and experience at a particular task have paid off and lead to the successful completion of previous projects. That may help you get assigned to tasks you feel most comfortable working on.

4. Intangibles: They Can Turn Into Tangibles

Every project involves things that we do not expect or see coming. It's those kinds of intangibles that can trip you up as they turn into tangibles. Anyone who has been in the business world for more then five minutes knows how delicate the process can be. Contractors show up to do a job, but have nothing to work with. A electricity brown out occurs just as you are ready to begin an important presentation. One or one hundred things can happen during a project to disrupt or slow things down. Developing alternative resources in advance can really save the day when push comes to shove.

5. Deadlines: Keep One Eye On A Deadline and The Other On Quality

Most companies live and die on deadlines. However, good companies and business leaders know that sometimes a deadline must be sacrificed in favor of quality over substance. Just having a finished project is not always a good thing is it means that the end result is substandard or will reflect on the company or team in a negative way. Every team leader and member should keep one eye on the deadline and the other on quality.

6. Learn From Your Mistakes

People and project teams that are set in their ways tend to make the same mistakes over and over again. If you are part of that kind of mess and know better, don't be afraid to have your objection on the record when you see the team headed in a direction that has proven disastrous on previous occasions. Moving forward in a positive way means being willing to try new directions instead of getting mired in flawed ideas that haven't worked well in the past.

7. Be Systematic, But Flexible

When it comes to successfully completing a business project, sticking to the plan is an essential. That kind of systematic approach keeps all the team members on track and working from the same playbook. However, there are times when a plan simply doesn't anticipate the unexpected. A Team leader and members most be willing to take a chance and bend the rules, occasionally, to get the job done.

8. Reign In The Personalities, Be Consistently Good

Most college graduates suffer from Professoritis. They take on the personality, mannerisms or management style of an Educator they admired while in school. This can be very bad news for co-workers because the style they have adopted is usually a harsh and unforgiving one. They tend to wear themselves and everyone else out. That makes it almost impossible for a team that must work together on a regular basis to function properly. Being consistently good means having the ability to manage and control yourself and your team. That includes gaining and retaining the respect of your peers. Someone with an over-bearing personality or completely out of control ego will always be a divisive force on any team.

9. Project Echoes: The Post-Project Meeting

Most team members are so glad to see a project completed that they rarely conduct a post-project meeting for fear it will turn into a blame fest. It doesn't have to be that way. A productive post-project meeting should explore the positives of what happened during the process. It's an opportunity to make a short list of new directions, shortcuts, resources and ideas that contributed to the success of a project. If a project failed to meet expectations, that's a matter for another day.

Surviving a project is all about professional etiquette and skill. It you do not have the skill necessary to be a productive part of any business team, blaming others or creating division among members will not help your cause. If you do possess the skills needed to help bring a project home, you also have the responsibility to work with other team members in and productive and civil way. Those willing to work with instead of against team members are often the voices of reason within a group. It's those people who end up reaping the most rewards.

Chapter Five: Career Building: Pink Elephants verses Purple Cows

Despite complex corporate structures and tens of thousands of small companies, there are really just two types of businesses these days. There are those that conform and those that do not. Conformist companies are looking for people who will say that elephants are pink if that's what management wants. Non-conformist businesses want employees who can think out of the box and create a purple cow if one is needed.

When it comes to career building, the best company to work for is one with a solid business identity. Those that cross over from conformist to non-conformist and visa versa tend to seek big personnel changes. That's bad news for most of the employees hired with the previous identity in mind. These situations usually occur when buyouts or takeovers cause a major change in a company's business philosophy.

In the uncertain business climate created by unpredictable world events and wild economic trends, building a career can be tough. There are probably a lot more jobs on your resume then you wish were there. However, I'll let you in on a little secret. It's become a trend within the business world to prefer people who have been beat up a bit due to corporate change. Those people are survivors who can provide invaluable experience and morale building insight if sudden change comes to a company.

When considering the direction your career will take, ask yourself where you will fit in the corporate scheme of things? Do you want to be an out of the box thinking purple cow designer? Alternatively, would you feel more comfortable in a company that sets strict limits on creativity? The answer may not come easy. One could argue that the market for purple cow people is always there, but only real geniuses need apply.

We've all met people who are self-labeled innovators. While their ideas may be inventive, they may also be highly impractical. When I meet them, I always hope they have large trust funds or a wealthy uncle not long for this world. While it's healthy to believe in yourself, it's unhealthy to avoid facing reality. If you want to work as a member of any corporate or business team, you have to fit in. Even the most creative and innovative person must be willing to accept constructive criticism and management's direction.

Most innovators discover their talent in the workplace, not prior to it. It may be that you'll have to work in a more structured environment until an opportunity to unleash your creativity arises. The key is being ready when that time comes! Part of that means being willing to be mentored and trained. It's often argued that people who attend coaching or training sessions really do not need it, while others who should be there are not. That's because those who attend value and profit from what they learn. Those who do not show up lose the opportunity to gain from the experience of others.

There is some truth to the argument that the most innovative people start their own companies. However, it may also be true that such people do so out of necessity. Many are unable or unwilling to work with or for others. This forces them to create their own job and some do so with great success. That's the good news if they are as good as they believe themselves to be. The bad news is that the vast majority of such people often go through a number of business failures before they actually find something that works for them and can turn a profit. The lesson learned is that innovative people who are willing to be trained and mentored are likely to be more successful in the end.

If you want to knock management over with new ideas, it would be wise to avoid companies looking for cookie-cooker employees. On the other hand, you may want to avoid start-up companies looking for the next Bill Gates. Until Bill signs on, funding can dry up and the pavement is not a fun place to be with bills to pay. Sometimes you can be fortunate enough to come across well-established companies with departments that still encourage creativity. While you may not find a Starbucks or Zen Garden in the coffee room, there may be enough wiggle room for some honest out of the box thinking. A situation like that can help propel someone willing to try it to the next level.

Corporations like to believe that they know exactly whom they are looking for when it comes to hiring the right people. However, anyone interested in building a successful career would be foolish to leave it up to a persuasive recruiter. Even the most promising positions can have very deep sinkholes hidden in the fine print. Before you take the plunge, decide if you're ready to see pink elephants, create purple cows or exist somewhere in between until better real opportunity knocks at your door.

Chapter Six: Effectively Delivering Your Message

Whether you're preaching a sermon, trying to sell something or wanting to nail down that presentation, delivery is everything. The best way to successfully deliver any message is to keep it fresh, keep it short, keep it simple and keep it fun.

When I started developing my first slide show years ago, I paused to reflect on what was right or wrong with most presentations. Placing one slide up on the screen and talking for an hour was something I didn't want to do. I had seen that same mistake made over and over in high school and college. The only things more boring then bad slide presentations are chalk talks and object lessons.

People new to speaking often depend on gimmicks. They often feel more comfortable using chalk board, an overhead projector, audience giveaways or something they can hold in their hand or place on a lectern for people to focus on. While these kinds of things can be useful in some cases, they can also be a distraction. A professional Speaker should never create a gap between themselves and their audience. You can steer clear of that pitfall by limiting the use of gimmicks and avoiding topic saturation.

The worst classroom nightmare that can happen to a junior or senior high school student is to end up with a teacher fresh out of college. They are easy to spot because of a misplaced passion to teach everything they have ever learned in one semester and burn up more chalk then a cheap ice cream company. Saying too much about any topic is as bad as not saying enough. An overuse of presentation graphics and technology detracts from your subject.

While tools like PowerPoint are a blessing to Speakers who were once chained to cumbersome and often unreliable slide projectors, they are not a substitute for content. Content will always be king. Editing content is an art form that must be learned through experience. Like many Speakers, most of my early gigs were for community groups, service organizations and clubs. They were, needless to say, unpaid. However, those engagements were excellent proving grounds for my material and provided good opportunities for me to sharpen my speaking skills.

The best way to understand what's right or wrong with a presentation is audience reaction. No matter how much you know about any topic or how passionately you present it, the audience will decide whether or not your presentation deserves their attention. Getting that attention means editing and presenting your content to suit them.

You can grab on to your audience by focusing in on the most interesting aspects of any topic. Let's say your topic is CORN. Most people are not going to care about how many tons of it are produced by farmers each year or what it takes to get it to market. They have already seen that on the Discovery Channel ten times over. Tell them what they don't know about the crop. Focus in on unusual uses, unique growing methods and uncommon processing procedures. Inform your audience by entertaining them.

Maintaining audience interest means speaking WITH them, not AT them. An audience will judge you by the first twenty words that come out of your mouth. This doesn't mean that you have to begin with a joke or story, it just means you have to start with sincerity. Say what you feel, not what you know and NEVER reintroduce yourself. During the first five minutes of your presentation, you will either gain or lose your audience. Begin with the WHO, WHAT, WHEN, WHERE and WHY of your topic. Those old journalistic building blocks serve professional Speakers well.

If content is king, comfort rules! You cannot successfully deliver your message to a room full of uncomfortable people. Your audience should be comfortable in every way imaginable. More then a few event planners have felt my wrath when I found horrific conditions present at various Speaking venues. I learned, early on, to verify any and all essential equipment and set-ups the day before my arrival. Arriving at least two hours before my audience on the day of a presentation was also important. That allowed time for any quick fixes.

Every member of your audience must be able to clearly see you, hear you and view any screen or monitor comfortably. If seating is portable, rows should be kept short. People like the ability to come and go as needed. Chilled water must always be available. A good listener is a comfortable listener.

You cannot get your message across if no one understands what you are talking about. Speakers often justify boring presentations by claiming that listeners will not appreciate the topic if they are not given the 'big picture.' These are Speakers who imagine an audience filled with Intellectuals or Professionals who appreciate the highbrow approach and hang on their every word. Anyone who has ever attended an average Financial Planning or Real Estate Investment seminar knows how tragic and ineffectual this kind of presentation can be.

If some Speakers put too much into a presentation, others depend on fluff and sideshows leaving their audience with nothing but a momentary high to take home. There is a big difference between a coaching session and public speaking. Coaches put on a show and depend as much on audience participation as they do on hype to get a point across. Coaches create an event and motivate participants, while professional Speakers deliver a message and enlighten their audiences.

Most Speakers I have met live on credentials. They write their own introductions and hope to impress an audience with all kinds of educational and professional accomplishments. Few live up to their resumes. That's because the focus is on them, not their message. With the possible exception of personality cults or celebrities, most people come out to hear the MESSAGE and not the Messenger. Given that, your delivery of that MESSAGE had better be good!

Let's revisit the essentials. Keep your presentation FRESH, keep it SHORT, keep it SIMPLE and make it FUN. This is a delicate balancing act. While you never want people to feel cheated because you didn't say enough, it's no better to say so much that they end up with a headache from trying to take it all in. Likewise, you do not want them to perceive you as a novice because you over-simplified things, depended on gimmicks, told too many jokes or replaced popular material with new stuff just to keep it crisp.

Every professional Speaker must balance content, technique, technology and audience satisfaction. It's a comfort zone that you reach through trial and error. You'll know you are there when audiences accept, enjoy and appreciate your message.

Chapter Seven: Getting A Unique Business Idea Off The Ground

I recently visited a website for entrepreneurs. Most of these websites are merely extended ads for various vending machines, donut makers, carpet cleaning franchises and roofing processes. This one was designed for people who actually dream up and create their own businesses. The website

I'm talking about is Startupnation.com and it's definitely for serious entrepreneurs only. People looking for a quick buck and easy start up home business should pass on this website and keep looking. Through a series of short articles and tutorials, Startup points out what it takes to get a unique and very successful small business off the ground.

I admire the fact that Startup pulls no punches. Anyone wanting to take the plunge into the world of real Entrepreneurs will quickly discover that there are simply no substitutes for careful planning and flawless execution. Startup is one of the best websites for entrepreneurs that I have ever visited. However, most of the innovative and successful entrepreneurs who manage to create and profit from a totally unique company, product or service, do so largely without the help of business consultants. That's because the very nature of the true entrepreneurial spirit is a personal one.

I have no doubt that the people involved with Startup and most any other competent business consultants can provide invaluable help and advice to anyone starting a business. However, most creative entrepreneurs have ideas that are unlikely to be implemented by using the normal process. Apple Computer and Martha Stewart Online are good examples of entrepreneurial companies that defied the process to get going and still mystify most of the traditional business world.

Business people tend to think in terms of recognizable products, services and ideas. The entire structure of funding, designing, manufacturing and marketing anything new is built around products and ideas that are basically recognizable. Someone may create a new type of shoe, but it's still a shoe. Were personal computers recognizable in the 1976 when Jobs and Wozniak created their first? No one in the mainstream business world knew how to design, build or market them. This didn't stop Steve Jobs from creating Apple Computer. He simply moved around all the obstacles by creating his own path.

When most people think of Martha Stewart, it's difficult for them to explain exactly what it is that she's selling. Sure, there's magazines, books and lots of designer household stuff, but what Martha is really selling is Martha! While I'm sure people at her company hate to think about it, it's hard to imagine MSO without Martha's magnetic and charismatic personality leading it. However, since no one lives forever, I'm sure that there is a plan already in place to keep the entire thing going long after Martha moves on to that great garden party in the sky. Marta Stewart created a unique business mold for the future and made it work.

Traditional funding, designing, manufacturing and marketing plans often do not work with unique products and services. What does work is the public's desire to buy them. If a market exists, there's got to be a way to get there. The key is knowing the expected size of the market.

Despite my advice to the contrary, I have seen too many prospective business owners make classic mistakes. The biggest mistake is believing that you need an rented office or retail store to make you're new business work.

Jobs and Wozniak started Apple in a garage. Martha Stewart started her company in her own kitchen. Most very successful small and some very large companies started in a garage, apartment or basement. That's because the entrepreneurs involved knew the value of keeping it cheap. A new product or service has to be given time to grow. That growth can be cut short if non-essential bills for rented space or unnecessary frills overtake the startup budget. Having the passion to create a new business means also having the good sense to be sure your new product or service has a fighting chance to get to market.

Apart from making bad financial decisions, another quick new business killer is bad advice. If you have proof that the public wants and will eagerly buy your new product or service, do not allow anyone to steer you off the course. Life is full of people who make an art out of negativity. Many say NO just to say it. They automatically assume that everyone who refuses to fit into the traditional business mold will fail. If I listened to all the people who told me that it would be impossible for me to do something, I would never get out of bed in the morning. There are always going to be those who will write you off. As long as you don't write yourself off, there's a good chance for success.

Good advice is still essential to the creation of a new business. However, good advice doesn't always have to be paid or expensive advice. You would be surprised at the number of free resources available to someone trying to start their own business. The U.S. Small Business Administration online at http://www.sbaonline.sba.gov/ has some painfully honest and helpful resources, including loans. It also pays to investigate any local clubs or gatherings where entrepreneurial businesspeople meet. There are always a few individuals willing to help mentor someone trying to get a new business off of the ground. However, it's wise to remember that no one will ever be as committed to your business idea as you.

When preparing a business plan, be flexible. Unexpected opportunities creep up when you least expect them. There are more then a few multi-millionaires out there who discovered they had a knack for doing something they hated and did it until they could fund their own business idea. If you discover a way to cash in on something else while trying to get your own unique product or service up and running, do not be afraid to take advantage of it. Anyone can put together the standard mom and pop store and have the doors open in a short period of time. Creating a business around a unique product or service is going to take a lot longer. You still have to eat and pay your bills while trying to make your dream com true.

Depending on your situation, it's unwise to expect your new business or product idea to be able to financially support you for some time. Have something to fall back on and be patient. Most great ideas take on a life of their own, travel at their own pace and require time to implement. Making quick decisions based on financial need is always a mistake. It's like people who take out a mortgage on their home to pay the unsecured debt on credit cards. If you do not pay your card bills, they'll send you nasty letters, ring your phone off the wall and damage your credit rating. However, you'll still have a place to live. It's all about making wise decisions that will move your business idea forward. Such decisions rarely help an entrepreneurs immediate financial situation.

Innovation, persistence, flexibility, common sense, patience and fiscal restraint are the best tools any potential new business owner can have. If you do not have those things, get them! Be prepared to travel on the road rarely taken and give yourself the benefit of the doubt. Most new unique products or services are not an instant success. However, those in it for the long haul often see their business and financial dreams come true.

Chapter Eight: Is Your Business A Dysfunctional Family?

The other day I brought my mother into an appliance store to purchase a television. By the time we left with her new television, she was completely disgusted. Unlike most of us, she comes from an older generation that actually expects salespeople and store employees to think of customers as valued visitors that represent their primary source of income. I wish that I could say that the store we visited was the exception, however, it was more the rule.

From the time we entered the store, we noticed that the salespeople and employees were not attentive to the needs of customers. They acted as though they were being bothered or disturbed when we asked for help. None were able to provide any information about what was actually included with the televisions that interested us. When we did finally decided on a TV, no one seemed interested in helping us. Finally, a very annoyed employee found the TV we were looking for and all but tossed it in our cart. To make matters worse, another employee was extremely annoyed that we had asked for help in lifting the large item into my vehicle.

After I brought the television to my mother's residence, we found that it didn't come with a coaxial cable or antenna. That was one of the questions the appliance store employees couldn't or didn't seem interested in answering. If the experience of being in that store hadn't been so negative, I probably would have been focused enough on the product to remember to buy a coaxial cable just in case it didn't come with one. I also forgot about several other smaller electronic items I had planned to purchase. My local Radio Shack benefited from the rudeness of those appliance store employees. They got the sale of the coaxial cable and a bunch of other things I needed. In retrospect, I probably should have just went there to begin with.

It's rare for most any customer or client to enter a retail or other business environment that operates like a well oiled machine. Instead, they are almost immediately confronted with poorly trained, incompetent and ill-mannered employees. This can be true whether the business is a small print shop, care dealership, insurance agency, professional's office or retail store. The store where we didn't receive the 'best' service happened to be part of a national chain of retail appliance stores. I've leave it up to you to figure out which one that was.

Despite the inconvenience and frustration associated with receiving less then acceptable treatment as a customer, there's a lot any current or prospective business owner or manager can learn from such an experience. The most important lesson is that when it comes to business, everything starts at the top. If the owner or manager of a business is not providing strong positive leadership, that company will be a nightmare for clients or customers.

The dream of every business owner or manager is to hire people who are self-starters that can function without constant supervision, while still keeping the company marching orders in mind. The nightmare of every business owner or manager is to find out that most of their employees do not fit into that category. Even if they did, leaving them alone is always a big mistake. Employees left to themselves are like children ignored by their parents. They go wild and do exactly as they please.

Whether we like it or not, every business owner or manager is like a parent. None can have the luxury of walking into their office, closing the door and hoping that everything outside of their little administrative world is going fine. On the other hand, holding sales or business meetings at the expense of customers trying to make a purchase or receive services is also a bad idea.

There is nothing more frustrating for a customer trying to make a purchase or solve a problem then to be told that their only connection to the business entity they are trying to deal with is in a meeting. I have been to car dealerships where salespeople were in a meeting when I tried to purchase a vehicle. I have been to stores where employees were in a meeting when I tried to get more information on a particular item. I have even found that my Veterinarian's sudden need to hold a meeting with his employees in the middle of a business day was the reason that my dog wasn't going to been seen.

One of the standard service jobs that I worked while trying to survive college was at a fast food restaurant. Despite the dreary nature of a job like that, I actually enjoyed working there. It was all about the Management. They were friendly, smart, personable and showed legitimate concern for their employees. It wasn't unusual for the Manager of that restaurant to jump on the grill on busy nights and lend a helping hand. However, the thing I remember and admire most about her was that she would host a Sunday breakfast every week for any employee that cared to attend. Schedules would be rotated so that everyone had a chance to sit down to a nice breakfast and join the give and take discussion.

Those Sunday meetings were fun, informative and motivational. However, the manager did more then just give pep talks or listen to employee suggestions. Because her restaurant was part of a network of other fast food establishments, she outlined how anyone could move up to management and build a career. That was more then just rhetoric. Almost all of the managers working in that particular restaurant had come up from the ranks. More importantly, all of us felt like we were part of a close family that we could count on for support. It's vitally important for sales people and employees to feel that way.

If a business owner or manager is merely some administrative hack, the entire company will be infected with the same sort of apathy. There is just no substitute for getting involved. This doesn't mean micromanaging, it simply means taking the time to be sure things are going well when they are supposed to be. It's been my experience that most business owners or managers are absent or preoccupied with something else when things are at their busiest. When some do show up, their presence is met with disgust or anxiety by employees. Instead of being team leaders, those kinds of bosses are considered armchair generals who are disrespected by their employees.

Unfortunately, even people who are strong team leaders have to sometimes lay down the law. No one can be a successful business owner or manager by being everybody's friend. There are times when conflicts with employees or customers will arise. The way you handle those conflicts will help define your effectiveness. Your job is to not to rubber stamp everything a customer says or an employee does. Instead, you should do everything possible to keep them from getting frustrated, angry or feeling ignored. That's when major conflicts erupt and tempers flare.

Most of the problems that develop between management and employees involve pay, time or job performance issues. Many of these problems can be avoided by proper attention to those areas of concern. An employee who has to worry about receiving the proper pay or being credited with the correct amount of time they worked is one that will not have their mind on their work. At the time of hire, a new employee should receive a full and comprehensive explanation regarding the procedure for making sure they are properly paid and their part in it. Likewise, they should be made to understand what is expected of them during a typical workday.

Chapter Nine: Is Your Professional Office Anything But...?

It's the nightmare that everyone who has ever been to a medical, dental or veterinary office fears more then having a tooth pulled or watching a doctor snap on some plastic gloves. It's the unprofessional, professional office. Those of us who have had the misfortune to be caught in that seemingly unending circle of waiting and filling out forms can attest to the sheer torture of such an experience. However, it doesn't have to be that way and there are some simple steps that every professional office can take to lesson the pain.

In an effort to limit the liability factor faced by every Medical Doctor or Dentist, referrals have become a way of life for them and endless nightmare for most patients. The situation for patients is exasperated by the need to fill out a deep pile of forms for every visit to every office. Some doctors and dentists try to ease the hassle by sending along patient information. Others try and have their receptionists procure as much information over the phone as practical. These are good first steps, but there are more practical ways to accomplish the same thing.

While not everyone has computer access or wants it, most people do. This opens up a simple way to save valuable office and personnel time. I have noticed a growing number of professional medical, dental and veterinary websites that offer online registration for real world services. Imagine the office and personnel time these professionals save, not to mention the pressure taken off their prospective patients. Just the freedom of being able to walk into a medical, dental or veterinary office without facing the prospect of filling out any number of mind-numbing forms is like chicken soup for the brain.

After the flu recently took up residence in our home, there was a need for several of us to visit the doctor. Since all of us were feeling poorly, an urgent medical care facility seemed to be the easiest way to obtain the services we needed. Despite being a good alternative to Hospital Emergency Rooms and Trauma Centers, urgent care centers can still frustrate those trying to use them. My last visit to one involved lots of forms and lots of waiting. Hoping for something better, I went online and started looking for more choices in my area.

After locating a new facility that had just opened near my home, I visited their website. I was immediately impressed by easily accessible contact information and online registration. In less then five minutes I was able to call them, talk to a live person and print up their patient registration form. Once there, I noticed that the place operated like a well-oiled machine. Everyone knew their job and did it well. No excessive waiting to be examined and very fast check out. There is nothing more frustrating then waiting an hour or more to check out and get the prescriptions you need to have filled after waiting hours to be examined.

The facility I visited for medical care was a good model for how things should work in any professional medical, dental or veterinary office. Sadly, it's the exception rather then the rule.

While many professional offices do not intentionally inconvenience their patrons, they simply do not use all the tools at their disposal. Most should begin by having fully functional websites with online registration and active email contacts. Imagine the office and personnel time that could be saved if potential patients could register online or ask questions via email. This is especially helpful if a question requires a direct consult with the doctor, dentist or veterinarian. This would free up the office phone for appointments and allow the professional to optimize his time beyond just returning calls to answer questions that could be dealt with by email.

If filing out forms in an office and waiting for treatment are primary pet peeves of most patients, dealing with phone answering systems is next on their list. Automated phone systems were supposed to be a way to build a bridge between the customer and the business, but many have simply become a frustrating wall for both. That's because most of these systems offer too many options and no quick route to live phone help. They try to combine an answering system for employees with a contact number for the public. If potential customers or patients cannot reach a live person 10-20 seconds into the call, they will probably hang up.

Despite spending thousands of dollars on computers loaded with software suited to their situation, most professional offices expect their employees to learn on the job. This places their valued patients, clients and customers in the hands of every new face that happens to come along. Most get frustrated and end up asking for the office manager or someone with whom they are more familiar. Every professional office or business of any kind is only as strong as the people who represent him or her on the phone or behind the reception desk.

Most professional offices of any size need competent office managers who know what needs to be done and gets results. Those results include scheduling enough appointments to keep the office profitable and getting patients in and out quickly. While paperwork, employee training and examination area preparation are unavoidable, they are not problems that patients should have to deal with.

Having more employees is not always the answer. I know a number of professionals who host a never-ending string of unpaid or low pay interns in their offices. Most of them come from local high schools or colleges and are there for the experience. These people get in each other's way, have no commitment to the professional and usually last less then a month before quitting. Meanwhile, the reputation of the professional is constantly being compromised.

Office preparation is a tool that should never be ignored by any professional. It's all too common to see patients waiting in their cars as the first employee to arrive places their key in the office door. Patients are there, but computers, office machines and other essentials are not anywhere near ready to go. It is equally common and unacceptable to see professional offices closed for cleanings, software updates and any number of other things that could and should be dealt with during hours when the office is closed.

The ever-growing number of professionals serving even the smallest of areas testifies to the fact that many people feel no loyalty to their doctor, dentist or veterinarian. While any medical, dental or veterinary professional will always have their fair share of one time, visiting or flaky patients, the lack of professionalism in many of their offices is creating a whole generation of visitors. All they really want is a doctor, dentist or veterinarian who will provide them with professional services in an efficient environment.

Chapter Ten: Move On and Move Up

The idea of competition has been well hidden in the politically correct world we are all forced to live in, but it's alive and well. Someone is going to win and it might as well be you! However, first you have to resolve the various issues that may be clouding your vision for a successful career.

Film dramas from the 1950's and 1960's often painted the suited American Worker as an office ant that was merely a cog in a larger machine. Every worker was characterized as being stuck in some impossible rut, being hassled by the boss and estranged from his or her family because of the job. This was the beginning of the idea that work is a bad thing.

More then a few nations have become prisoners of their own social politics. They have shorter workdays, shorter workweeks and economic problems that get worse every year. Why? Because they have bought into the lie that there is something wrong with working hard and becoming a success.

It's no easy thing to balance time with loved ones and work hours. However, it's wrong to believe that one has to win and the other loses. We all have to work and there is just no getting around the fact that those who put out the extra effort will win the prize. The key to balancing family and work is to make sure that you are not the only one trying to pull off a successful balancing act.

I cannot tell you how many times I have come across people who are made to feel guilty because they have to work. Wives, husbands, partners and children do what they want, when they want, then chide their better half or parent for spending too much time on the job. What about them?

When's the last time your other half planned an evening out, made reservations or did anything other then complain? What about the kids? Are they willing to give you and your other half a break so you can go out? Would the world end if your older children gave up a trip to the Mall or a sports practice for a family evening out or some babysitting duty?

If family or partners aren't your problem, perhaps you are? There are all sorts of personal issues that can easily overcome us if we allow it. The idea is to identify the problems we have or mistakes we're making and correct those behaviors. If you're trying to start a career, this is an essential step. Let's start with education.

More then a few people linger too long in the world of academics because they have been told that the real world is just too tough to master without the proper educational credentials. A better alternative is going to school while you go to work. Running back to school to avoid a job search or potential employment is a common and often foolish mistake.

The real world is no harder or easier then school, but it's certainly more rewarding. At some point, you have to decide to move on and start your working life. Unless you are independently wealthy, you are going to school on the government dime. Those loans have to be paid back, a fact that is easily forgotten until the notices start arriving in the mail. Like any other financial decision, the amount you spend on educational loans has to pay off for you in the end. One advantage to going to school while you work are the numerous tuition rebate, assistance and full payment plans that many companies now offer.

Once you are working, the key to getting ahead is moving up. If you do not move up, someone else will move you out. Work is all about competition and that's not a bad thing. The key to winning that competition is attitude monitoring. Most of us worry more about our physical health then we do our mental health. It is for that reason that so many people find themselves enslaved to anti-depressants and designer attitude drugs. They cannot control their attitude, so they allow a drug to do it.

Before you run to Doctor Feelgood for your next script, take an inventory of your feelings. It is not what makes us feel good, but what causes you to feel bad that we often ignore. Things like guilt, unresolved conflicts and regret often eat at us like internal parasites and refuse to allow us the privilege of enjoying our lives. Well, unless you want to spend the rest of your life as a human pill bottle, you have to confront these matters and move on.

Take a mental photo of yourself. Look for the things that are making you feel bad and seek to resolve them. It's true that we cannot control everything in our lives, but we can fight back against the kind of external forces that threaten our happiness. Left to themselves, things like guilt, unresolved conflicts and regret can lead to unhappiness, depression and all sorts of bizarre phobias and abnormal behaviors.

Once you have your mental house in order, become a master of your self. The most successful people in the world are those that predetermine their behavior. Decide in advance how to respond to negative people, comments, insults and confrontations. This will prevent anyone who tries to mow you over from doing so. It will also send a message to those you work or do business with. They will understand that you are a person in charge of yourself and a force to be reckoned with.

The whole concept behind competition is to win. However, everyone has his or her own way of doing that. Do not try to copy someone else's success by being them. Learn from others, but never try to duplicate exactly what they do. Develop a plan for success based on your own positive attributes and strengths. Once you get rid of the negative things in your life, learn to manipulate the positive side of yourself and move up.

Chapter Eleven: Residual Income Schemes: Will They Make You Rich?

We've become a society of wealth seekers. Inspired by persons like Donald Trump, Bill Gates and Martha Stewart, people are lining up to join the Billionaire Club. Like these wealthy role models, Billionaire Wannabees hope to achieve their lofty financial goals by hanging their success on a specific industry, product or idea. Other opportunists are seeing their own finances grow by providing what appears to be a fast track to earning big bucks.

Residual income schemes are everywhere. You cannot turn on your television, listen to the radio or check your email without being overwhelmed by ads for Get Rich Quick plans. For just a couple of hundred to many thousands of dollars, these schemes claim that they will help you secure your financial future in short order. Most offer to teach you how to flip real estate, sell in volume on Ebay, market health products, operate a fleet of vending machines or own your very own bunch of ATMs. But which one will make you rich and do it in record time?

Unlike investment seminars that are designed to help the financially comfortable and already wealthy to get richer, most of these programs are directed at people who want out of their work-a-day world. They promise a means to escape the drudgery of boring jobs and never-ending financial problems. Sadly, few are able to deliver. But not all of it is their fault.

Choosing one of these 'wealth building systems' as they are known, requires a level of commitment that is equal to starting a small business. That commitment can be financial, as well as physical. It's unreasonable to expect a part-time business to provide full time income. If that's what you're looking for, it doesn't exist. If it did, we would all be doing it. Before committing to any one of the get rich quick schemes, you have to decide if they measure up to real world standards beyond all the hype.

Flipping real estate purchased with no money down is one of the most popular schemes out there. Enlightened real estate investors discovered this method during economic downturns experienced over the past forty years. While it still works today, this is for people who are handy when it comes to basic repairs, know how to spot and obtain distressed properties with some value and have no problem with mountains of paperwork. If you are not ready to deal with the occasional legal hassles and able to accept all the financial risks involved, walk away from this.

Ebay has managed to become the parent to all kinds of get rich quick schemes. From courses that promise to make you a successful Power Seller to brick and mortar shops that accept items to be sold on the auction website, Ebay schemes are everywhere. Most, however, have come along too late. While Ebay remains the biggest auction Website in the world, it has become a place where too many people are trying to sell the same wholesale items. Second hand and used goods have also lost their glamour unless they are highly sought after antiques or collectibles.

Health, beauty and household products have always been used as a way to establish and build a second income. Mary K, Amway, Tupperware and Avon are good examples of programs that work and offer varying levels of income. If you're a good salesperson, have a big family and lots of friends, you can make some money by selling their products part-time. For those who want to earn more, most of these companies offer sponsorship programs. How much more depends on your ability to enlist motivated people. The real cash doesn't come from selling lipstick and storage containers. It comes from signing up a few hundred others to sell under your supervision and then getting them to sign up people to sell under their supervision.

Examples of the worst of get rich quick schemes are the ATM and vending machine offers. Slick promotional packages and smooth presentations have thousands of people investing their nest eggs in electronic machine franchises each year. These Investors should have talked to all the people who lost thousands investing in privately owned pay phones and refurbished video games before they signed on the dotted line. The technology may have changed, but the hassles are the same.

The concept is sound enough, but the plan is flawed. People will purchase lottery tickets, phone cards, food and beverages, candy, disposable cameras and even rechargeable cell phones from vending machines. They use machines to purchase and rent DVDs, buy music CDs, develop film or get extra digital prints and create custom greeting cards. Then there are the ATMs. People are always going to need some cash, right? The sales pitch is that most people feel more comfortable using a vending machine or ATM inside a business then along a roadside late at night or early in the morning. They want YOU to be the owner of one of those machines inside a store, hotel or restaurant.

More then a few Innkeepers and Restaurant Owners have already fallen victim to illegitimate candy, food, lottery ticket, cell phone and snack machine scams. After spending thousands of dollars with the idea of placing these little moneymakers in their establishments, they ended up losing their investments. Some were shipped cheap machines that never actually worked or broke after a couple of uses. Others never received any equipment at all and having fallen victim to fly by night criminals.

Beyond brick and mortar store, restaurant and retail business Owners, the biggest targets of electronic machine schemes are people who have forty to five hundred thousand dollars to invest. They are promised premium machines, products and locations. In some cases, those making these offers are legitimate companies willing to deliver exactly what they promise. However, most machines purchased from these companies are priced far above their actual value and ability to produce a reasonable profit.

Despite being portrayed as a part-time opportunity that will produce a substantial return on the investment, vending machines require full time maintenance and can have a very high down time rate if not constantly attended. And there are lots of hassles. Broken and vandalized machines, disagreements over profit splits with business owners and over-priced machine merchandise. I have never known a single small investor who was able to make any money from privately owned or leased ATMs or vending machines. Conversely, I have known plenty who ended up putting in twelve to sixteen hour days servicing machines to enrich others.

Many smaller investors seek their pot of gold online. Apart from the moral issues and legalities involved, investors are often taken in by porn and gambling Website schemes. Most are over-priced investment sinkholes that will leave their owners with endless checking account debits and little or no profits. The successes of these schemes are dependent on volume. Unless you have lots of online friends willing to pay up to see nudity or place their bets on a Website with a clear house advantage, you are not going to make any money. Instead, you are likely to lose more than your initial investment with locked-in monthly fees and contract expenses.

Most get rich quick schemes will not provide the results you're looking for. The key to making a residual income through marketing is finding a niche. You need to offer people something they want, are willing to pay for and cannot easily find elsewhere. Sometimes that niche is not about selling a new or unique item, but taking an established product and making it easier or more convenient for people to buy. The same is true of service. People appreciate fast, friendly service. Making money is about being smarter, working harder and competing more aggressively than the rest.

Chapter Twelve: The Apprentice Is a Tough Love lesson In Workplace Relationships

Some educators encourage their students to watch whatever incarnation of The Apprentice happens to be available hoping they will pick up on some of the methods, ideas and solutions presented. Others write the show off as a series of staged events that offer nothing in terms of business education. Both viewpoints have valid arguments, but they are missing the real lessons offered by Donald Trump's reality television show.

The Apprentice is a must-see for anyone who desires to master the art of workplace relationships. Whether producer Mark Burnett and his crew egg-on contestant feuds and squabbles behind the scenes as some claim are less important then the disagreements themselves. They typify the problems that come into play when egos, sexuality, personalities, experience, flirtations, age and education collide in the workplace.

The whole idea of The Apprentice is a fascinating one. People have to work together in teams for the ultimate benefit of just one member. That concept is acted out in real life everyday within the corporate workplace. Everyone is trying to climb the same ladder and it can get pretty crowded at times. The lessons to be learned from The Apprentice are how to remain on the ladder and eventually make it to the top.

The television show makes it easy to spot those used to working as part of a team and the others who can't. It also exposes the various agendas and temporary alliances created to remove undesirable or threatening team members. These are the things you should pay attention to and learn from. Just trying to avoid being someone's target in the corporate workplace is an art form in itself.

There are some obvious solutions to workplace relationship problems that are amply illustrated on The Apprentice. One is the simple concept of Mentoring. As with the television show, a good Mentor is not going to think and act for you. Instead, they are going to guide you in the right direction and give you some straight talk when you screw up. This is what Donald Trump does. Martha Stewart is more polite, but no less forceful in her incarnation of The Apprentice.

Both television shows illustrate the importance of learning to listen. When in a meeting, receiving instructions from a project manager or getting advice from a Mentor, you must be sure that you are listening to what is being said. If you cannot understand the goal, you can't reach it. During the first episode of the Martha Stewart Apprentice, Martha clearly spelled out the ultimate goal of the first project. It was to see how well each team could connect with their customers. The team that failed never had that simple goal in sight to begin with.

Donald Trump is always concerned as much with his image as he is with making money. For him, the two are one, no goal rises above that and he is easily able to communicate this to team members. Despite that, we have seen many examples where teams simple ignore the Trump philosophy in trying to complete their tasks. This leads to failure and firing. Part of surviving the real life corporate workplace means being able to sign on to a corporate philosophy and embed it in everything you do.

Despite the desire to include a wealth of entrepreneurs within the Apprentice wannabees, most are used to being the boss rather then working under one. The successful entrepreneurs we've seen on The Apprentice are those who can marry their ability for creative thought with the need to work closely with others and treat them as equals. Perceptive team members know that the losers will fall off by their own hands. They understand the need to keep a low profile and wait for blowhards and frauds to self-destruct. Those who try to manipulate things by drawing attention to themselves on The Apprentice, usually end up on the short list of those soon to be fired. The same may be said to be true in real life.

American Culture has encouraged individualism for at least half a century. The idea that it's all about ME has become embedded in our education, religious, political and business systems. It's allowed the needless development of personality cults around bogus political, religious and business leaders in place of common sense. The results have been predictable, costly and unnecessary.

If Donald Trump and Martha Stewart can teach us anything, it's that even the most creative and charismatic people must work with a team to achieve their goals. That team should sign on to their philosophy, support their goals and benefit in every way they can from working in such an environment. Those who have come to compete for The Apprentice position and haven't arrived with a good grasp of real life workplace etiquette are unlikely to last long.

Success as part of any workplace team means putting aside personality conflicts, quick tempers and anything that can distract from the job at hand. Individual success often comes at the cost of being part of a successful team. The rewards can be substantial and it doesn't always pay to be the top dog. That is another lesson well taught by Donald Trump and Martha Stewart.

Chapter Thirteen: The Apprentice: Learning Lessons From Eccentrics

Recent incarnations of The Apprentice featured some very unusual people. While I'm sure they were chosen to spice up the show, none of them seemed to possess the skills or expertise needed to compete on that level. If the show was supposed to be all about people vying for a mega-management position with the Trump Organization, these were candidates with the wrong stuff for that much-coveted spot. While the show and more conventional candidates may not have benefited from the antics of these bizarre applicants, serious viewers can certainly profit from their mistakes and eccentricities.

Apprentice 3 gave us the amazing Danny. Looking like a leisure suit hippy, this guy loved to strum the guitar and sing. He had a gimmick, but couldn't seem to consistently deliver the goods as part of a team. Apprentice 4 introduced the often incomprehensible and seemingly ineffectual Markus. He became an outcast in the competition having proved to be uninspiring and frustrating to colleagues during various tasks. But my personal favorite was Brent from Apprentice 5. Here was a guy who loved to tell everyone about how much he would bring to the table. However, he didn't work and play well with others and became known more as a big eater than a heavyweight performer. To challenge him was to face a verbal barrage and witness his own special brand of temper tantrum.

When it came to working as part of a project team trying to successfully complete a challenging task, these characters forgot all about FLEXABILITY. As The Donald has often demonstrated, you don't have to compromise to be flexible. You just have to be willing to try a new approach, consult others with more expertise and go with the flow when you see that it benefits everyone involved including you. Instead, Danny, Markus and Brent became obstacles of their own creation. Each decided that every task would be approached from the standpoint of their own philosophy and methodology. This made them appear as unyielding and incompetent, even though all three had achieved a measure of success within their chosen careers.

Another important lesson to be learned from these three eccentrics is that being UNCONVENTIONAL is not always desirable when you're faced with a tough project and rapidly approaching deadline. In order to think outside of the box, you have to know what's inside. That means being familiar with time-proven techniques and procedures that have worked for others facing similar tasks. It also means being intellectually prepared. People with a passion for success will equip their mental toolbox with a willingness to learn and the ability to be consistent, intuitive, flexible, creative, decisive, unpretentious and motivated. If we judge them by their contributions to each task as Trump did in the boardroom, we see that Danny, Markus and Brent failed to exhibit evidence of these qualities which can help produce outstanding project team members and excellent leaders. While seeking to be his Apprentice, many candidates who compete on the show end up fired because they fail to follow the example set by Trump.

While most people think of Donald Trump as the ultimate Entrepreneur, he is also an astute businessperson. While he leads with authority and has no trouble getting his point across, Trump also inspires people with success and motivates them with opportunity. When it comes to moving his business empire forward, he doesn't just think about making money. Trump is always looking for new opportunities to make more money by providing the very best product or service to those who can afford it. With his name boldly emblazoned on and associated with everything he does from a business standpoint, Trump has to insist on a superior level of quality. As a successful innovator, The Donald is second to none.

The Apprentice unashamedly presents the good, bad and ugly of people competing in the workplace. It's a fantastic opportunity for success-driven individuals to learn the ABC's of business behavior. If there is one vital lesson to be extracted from that aspect of the show it is that being eccentric isn't a bad thing, as long as it doesn't make us own our worst enemy.

Chapter Fourteen: The Horror of WorkZilla (Or, How To Handle A Nightmare Employee)

Although self-employed for many years, I have been a regular visitor to workplaces small and large as a Business Consultant, Staff Trainer or Special Event Speaker. When the purpose for my visit has to do with business consultation, it doesn't take long for me to locate the biggest potential problem in any office. It's WorkZilla!

WorkZilla is a nightmare employee who instills a quiet fear in the workplace that causes productive employees to quit, stay home or just give up when it comes to deadlines or productivity. This monster is smart and knows how to exploit the system. Even if supervisors know about the problem, they are unlikely to report WorkZilla for fear of retribution. By the time upper management becomes aware of a WorkZilla in their midst, most of the damage is already done. This creature knows how to consolidate its power and create carefully planned barriers to prevent its dismissal.

WorkZilla isn't just smart; it's charming and often has many allies. Carefully winding its tentacles around the most emotionally or professionally vulnerable people within its sphere of influence, WorkZilla carefully builds a small group of dedicated supporters. This group is always ready, willing and able to counter any negative comments or complaints that might reach the ears of upper management. They become its first line of defense against administrative action.

Supervisors often find themselves between a rock and a hard place when it comes to WorkZilla. This nightmare employee creates a personality cult of peer support and hides behind any essential technical or other essential skills they may possess. Most nightmare employees manage to blackmail their supervisors by constantly reminding them how essential they are to any project. It's not unusual for WorkZilla to have more power and influence in the workplace then their immediate Supervisors.

Despite any technical or other indispensable skills a WorkZilla may possess, no workplace can function smoothly with one in their midst. There is always an ultimate price to be paid for allowing this creature to inhabit and flourish in any place of business. Besides creating an unpleasant and outright combative atmosphere, WorkZilla tends to reproduce. Once other employees see how this creature gets over on management, they learn by example and become workplace monsters in their own right.

WorkZilla is not the kind of creature that will respond to subtle hints. Trying to control it by sending employee behavior expectation and productivity memos to the entire office will meet with immediate failure. Such an action would merely create another tool that WorkZilla can use to consolidate its power and lower workplace morale. Any nightmare employee has to be directly confronted. Because WorkZilla has nothing but contempt for management, this confrontation has to be carefully planned and flawlessly executed.

Any confrontation must be based on facts, not here say. Simply rattling off a number of complaints from its peers will not be sufficient to take down WorkZilla. It would simply enlist an equal number of followers to discredit the whistle blowers. Complaints must be based on inappropriate behavior or actions that have been documented by upper management as they occur. This means that a period of observation and work evaluation will be needed before any confrontation is scheduled.

Immediate supervisors and upper management should conduct the confrontation and WorkZilla should be notified well in advance. Notification must be in writing and include a receipt signed by the nightmare employee and witnessed by at least one supervisor and a member of upper management. The purpose of the sit down must be clearly spelled out. That purpose is be to present specific allegations of violations of company rules, policies or workplace etiquette.

WorkZilla should be given the opportunity to chose an alternative meeting date or time within reason. The nightmare employee must be given an opportunity to respond to the allegations verbally or in writing shortly after the actual confrontation.

Once the confrontation is planned and WorkZilla is notified, the entire matter should be kept strictly confidential. WorkZilla should be informed that he or she is not to discuss the meeting or purpose of the meeting before or afterward with other employees. The only contact regarding the matter available to it should be a member of upper management. There must be a clear and immediate sanction available if WorkZilla discusses the matter with others in the workplace or refuses to attend the meeting.

The idea is to begin to socially isolate WorkZilla from other employees and make him or her aware that their reign of terror is coming to an end. Because most of these creatures have egos bigger then their ability to control a workplace, the average WorkZilla will probably throw in the towel and resign. However, you must remember that WorkZilla is also a kind of jailhouse lawyer that loves to exploit the system. You must be prepared to follow through with the meeting in case he or she doesn't leave.

Before you hold court against WorkZilla, make sure that everyone on your side of the table is on board with the agenda. That agenda isn't to create a lynch mob designed to take down WorkZilla. It's an organized effect on the part of management to restore order and increase productivity within the workplace environment that had been disrupted by an employee's inappropriate actions. The idea is to bring WorkZilla into the mainstream of accepted employee behavior. While it's doubtful that will happen, the last thing you need is for WorkZilla to perceive the meeting as a corporate witch hunt with him or her caught holding the broomstick.

Once WorkZilla is isolated from his or her support system of dedicated followers, the idea is to give this creature enough rope to hang itself. Removing its ability to manipulate the workplace and those in it is like taking drugs away from a drug addict. It's unlikely that WorkZilla will be able to cope with losing the power he or she has worked so hard to consolidate. Instead, they'll probably try and negotiate one final victory in the form of a lump sum payment designed to bribe them to resign. Paying WorkZilla to leave would be a mistake and send the wrong message to other potential workplace monsters waiting in the wings. It would be better to hold its feet to the corporate rulebook fire.

WorkZilla is not a problem exclusive to workplace management. It will attack other employees for any reason or none at all. If you find yourself facing WorkZilla on a daily basis, it's important to keep a logbook. You should carefully document any unnecessary sarcasm, insults or outright slander directed toward you (not others). Incidents of project sabotage or purposeful work disruption are likely to be of particular interest to upper management.

If you do decide to blow the whistle, be discreet. While it may seem wise to engage other employees in a discussion of WorkZilla and even ask them to join you when reporting this creature, that's exactly what you should not do. WorkZilla exists because it understands the system better then you do. Enlisting the help of other employees will merely cause it to bring on those who are part of its personality cult. In the end, you'll look like the villain instead of the victim.

WorkZilla's worst enemy is upper management. They are unlikely to be as intimidated as immediate supervisors. For them, it's all about productivity. If you can prove that good people are leaving, missing work or slowing down because of WorkZilla, its days will be numbered. When reporting incidents, carefully follow company rules and do not expect an immediate response. If you have been the victim of any sort of direct harassment or threat of physical violence by WorkZilla, report the matter to your company security office.

Chapter Fifteen: Think Before You Bank on the Web

When people first heard about Ebay, it seemed like a dream come true. For just a couple of bucks, you could list all your old stuff online and clean out that garage or attic without having bargain hunters invade your property. Small business owners also discovered Ebay and found that it was a great way to move items that weren't flying off the shelves. Artists and specialty item sellers found a home at the online auction site and a worldwide audience of potential buyers looking for just what they are selling. Entrepreneurs took the whole thing, ran with it and created some very successful businesses within a business.

Just when it seemed that Ebay was a dream comes true for almost anyone selling stuff, the website just got too big. All of a sudden, people found themselves paying huge fees for a featured listing. Without a featured listing in the correct category, you were just another seller among the millions. Such listing fees often ate up most of any potential profits to be made and offered no actual promise of success. Today, it seems that creating a listing on Ebay and paying the requested listing fees is akin to dropping coins into a slot machine. Welcome to the world of trying to make money online!

Most people laugh about web-based get rich quick schemes, but there is no place to make or lose money faster, except maybe the stock market. For better or worse, the nature of anything web-based is to get in on the ground floor, make your money and get out before too many others join the party. Anyone who banks long term on the web tends to lose. Just ask any of the once highly touted online marketing websites. The problem is that when they lose, they tend to take many people with them.

There is no doubt that anyone who has a legitimate item to sell needs to have it available online. The question is, "How much are you willing to spend to become an Ebay Power Seller, get a high sales ranking on Amazon or be listed somewhere in the top twenty on the search engines?" Whether you have a personal website or depend on some mega-shopping website to get your item out there, it's going to cost you some bucks to bring people to your product. So before you quit your day job and get ready to rack in all those big web bucks, make sure it will be worth your while.

Getting a product noticed on the web can be a very expensive lesson. More then a few online merchants invested all their efforts in one online marketing plan, made money and then lost big. Others never even made it out of the starting gate. Here are some simple ways to avoid complete online financial failure:

1. Never put all your eggs in one online shopping basket.

Do not depend on one website, one submission program or service, one e-shopping mega-listing site or one payment method for your online income.

2. Avoid digital products unless you're an expert.

Don't be taken in by reselling schemes to market useless reports. If you have life experience in a particular industry or expertise that others may be able to profit from, use it to your advantage. Create and market an ebook. Before you do, research the procedure, expected cost and profit potential.

3. If you can't sell soap to your neighbors, you will not sell it online.

Tens of thousands of people are taken in each year by extravagant plans to sell jewelry, medications, vitamins, cosmetics and household cleaning products online. Most of these people would not be a success trying to sell these things offline to neighbors and will not fair any better in the digital world.

4. Do not depend on Affiliate Programs for a substantial income.

Affiliate programs are a way to get a few extra bucks out of a popular website. A stable and fairly honest affiliate program like the one offered by Amazon.com is good. Some multi-merchant affiliate websites like Share-A-Sale are also worth a shot. Others may be geared to change once you start making any money, essentially robbing you of commissions due for sending motivated buyers to their merchants.

5. Sell unique or competitive products.

Don't be taken in by scams that get you to purchase a bunch of wholesale junk, and then try to sell it on Ebay. If you do plan on buying to resell online, do your homework. Find out who else is selling the same thing for how much they're charging. The most successful online merchants sell items that are unique or in such high demand that the market allows for a wide variety of sellers and prices.

6. Less clicks mean more customers.

The less complicated you make it for customers to purchase your products, the more you will sell. It's estimated that for every one click a customer executes to find or purchase your products, you can lose as little as ten or as many as one thousand sales. Make it easy for them, even if it's harder for you.

7. Expect the worst, enjoy the best.

A responsible real world merchant will be ready for major setbacks like natural disasters, thefts and personal injury lawsuits. Online merchants regularly face cancelled listings or withheld payments fueled by buyer complaints, website or payment processing outages and sudden search engine dropouts.

8. Selling is an art. Are you an artist?

Not everyone has the personality and skills needed to be a success at selling. Anyone who wants to sell online has to be able to translate his or her personality and skills into the digital world. If you are completely baffled by the internet and lack the time needed to learn what it's all about, becoming an online merchant would probably be a very bad idea.

The vast majority of people who try to make money online will never meet their own financial expectations. In most cases, the culprit will be poor planning. In others, bad execution. Overall, anyone planning a web-based business needs to approach his or her endeavor in a serious way. While optimism is always a good motivator, it cannot replace proper planning and risk assessment.

Chapter Sixteen: Vending Machines: Legitimate Investment or Get Rich Quick Scam?

Ads for amazing, entrepreneurial opportunities fill the airways. On many cable channels, infomercials touting get rich quick schemes have replaced those for cut through steel knives and pocket fishing gear. It's a sign of the economic times. Our Nation's population is getting older and many folks over fifty have surplus money to invest. Younger people, looking for a way to escape the daily grind, are eager to max out credit cards, withdraw their nest egg and cash in those savings bonds to start a profitable business. The problem with cookie-cutter opportunities of the type currently being offered is that they are designed to make someone else rich, not you!

Vending machines have been the darlings of entrepreneurial magazines and publications for the past twenty years. While ads for roof coating and carpet cleaning franchises, computer enhanced photo and donut machines attract some takers, most people respond to the vending machine opportunity ads because they require a smaller investment.

The majority of people who invested a few hundred to a few thousand bucks in these deals got stung badly. Many of the seemingly reputable vending machine offers came from fly by night scam artists. They would collect a pile of money, close down their operation after sending out a few cheap machines that never worked right and start up all over again under a different business name. Even some of the vending deals that were legitimate were anything but the lazy man's road to wealth.

Those who invested in vending machines, received their equipment and began to place them in stores and other high traffic areas were in for a rude awakening. Most found out later that they paid double or even triple what the machines were actually worth. Others were being soaked on the price of inventory and had trouble getting the supplies in time to fill their machines. But that was just the beginning of their woes.

I cannot tell you how many letters and emails I have received over the years asking me if I could offer some advice on how to get out of a vending business that was sucking the very life, in terms of money and time, out of its owner. People that had expected an easy second income out of their new vending business to make their car or house payments found themselves stuck in a bottomless money pit. Broken or vandalized machines quickly ate up profits. The time needed to service their investment was also a big problem. The few hours a week mentioned as a realistic commitment of time to run their new business turned out to fall short by double digits.

Many vending machine business owners that I heard from were close to total exhaustion. They found themselves spending from four to eight hours every night dealing with the machines after leaving their normal day job. Much of that time was pure loss as they had to repair machines and deal with irate store owners who were getting tired of customers complaining to them about money lost in damaged or defective equipment.

I recall one sad tale that came from a man in his sixties. He purchased some vending machines for a retirement income and quickly found himself out on the road from twelve to fourteen hours every day fixing, restocking and changing the location the machines. After several months of this, he had a heart attack. His brother kindly agreed to visit the vending route while the man recovered. A week went by before his brother could start the serving the route. When he did, he found that many of the stores where the machines were located had placed them in back rooms or even left them on the street. The merchants just couldn't deal with all the customer complaints.

A new generation of vending machines has arrived on the scene to replace the candy, gum, snack and convenience models. These are electronic machines that offer movies, internet access and even money. For the right investment amount, you can own your own video rental business, pay-per-use internet access terminal or ATM! Most people are smart enough to realize how much work it would be to refill DVD rental machines for the small profit margin offered, but many get taken in by the internet access or ATM machine offers. A significant investment is needed to own the internet access or ATM machines, but are the rewards as great as the offers claim?

With cell phones and laptop computers now offering more wireless internet access possibilities then even, the internet machines would be used by a very small section of the population. Many restaurants, businesses and hotels now offer free internet access. Some even provide computers. Libraries offers computers and the internet for free. Ask any large phone company why you see less and less pay phones in public areas? If they are honest, they'll tell you that it's all about cost verses return. It costs phone companies a fortune to service payphones. There are hundreds of thousands of fewer users because of cell phone popularity and the remaining payphones are always targets for vandalism, theft and free dialing scams.

Most of the ATMs being offered to private citizens through entrepreneur ads are really just psuedo-bank machines. Most dispense receipts instead of cash. The customer then has to take the receipt to the store owner and get their cash. This makes more work for the store employees and provides hassles for the machine owner. The return is usually less then a dollar per transaction. The selling point to the store is supposed to be that customers who can get more money will spend it in their store. The problem is that most stores sign agreements with local companies offering real ATMs that dispense cash and provide little or no hassles for the store owner or employees. Why would they want yours?

Most of the new electronic machines are less likely to be vandalized because they make sales or transactions using credit cards, not cash. But that advantage can quickly vanish if you have to have to deal with merchant account providers. Many will hold back funds from credit card transactions to protect themselves from charge backs if you do more then a certain amount of business each month. The same is true of companies offering so-called easy to get or 100 percent approval merchant accounts and credit card systems that allow you to accept cards for items or services you sell online.

I have watched the entrepreneurial vending machine business for over twenty years and have yet to meet or hear from one satisfied customer. There are ways to purchase, own, supply and service vending machines that are far less expensive and more legitimate then by responding to a late night cable television or magazine advertisement. People who own legitimate vending machines will tell you that it's not an easy road to riches and requires the establishment of a good system of support that is beyond the financial scope of most individuals.

Chapter Seventeen: Wayne Rogers: From Actor To Super Investor

It took a tragedy not far removed from Wayne Rogers to wake him up when it came to money and how to handle it. According to an interview he gave to the Financial Intelligence Report, Wayne had first met Peter Falk when the two shared a room in New York City. Falk, an accomplished film, stage and television actor, later suffered a financial trauma not uncommon to many other celebrities.

In the 1970s while both the longtime friends were living and working in Hollywood, Peter Falk became a victim of fraud. Falk lost around $250,000 to a crooked business manager and he wasn't alone. Bad investments had claimed the fortunes of many of Hollywood's Elite.

John Wayne almost went bankrupt due to bad investments. Bud Abbot of Abbot and Costello spent his last days dying of cancer and flat broke in Woodland Hills, California. Poor money management and a huge IRS bill claimed the fortunes of both members of the famous comedy team. Jackie Coogan earned over four million dollars as a child star in the 1920's, but lost all his money to his mother and stepfather who had invested badly and wasted the rest on a lavish lifestyle.

These lessons on how celebrities had handled their money were a wake up call to Wayne. He began looking into the world of investing and started his financial empire by purchasing apartment buildings in foreclosure. Rogers started investing with a simple goal in mind. He wanted to hold on to his money and make it grow. He later moved on from real estate to stocks and bonds.

Wayne Rogers has had a distinguished acting career having appeared in films like Cool Hand Luke and Ghosts of Mississippi, as well as having played the unstoppable Capt. John Francis Xavier 'Trapper John' McIntyre in M*A*S*H from 1972-1975. He still makes movies and appears on television, but he has also become a superstar in another genre. Rogers has become a force to be reckoned with among the elite of super investors.

Wayne Rogers can frequently be seen on Fox News giving investment advice that people are eager to follow. He prefers mutual funds because they limit risk, but also likes commodities. Like many investors, he watches the state of the economy and the performance of individual companies. When it comes to choosing stocks, Rogers prefers many and says that company earnings are the key to deciding which to buy because they drive stock prices.

Charismatic, well-spoken and funny, Wayne Rogers has succeeded in two of the world's most difficult professions: Acting and Investing. The lesson he teaches us is a simple one based on his original investing goal: Hold on to your money and make it grow!

Chapter Eighteen: Better Communication Techniques: Do You Sound Like A Broken Record?

Phrases and quotes come in and go out of style with each generation. When I was growing up in the 1960's, people described those who liked to continually repeat themselves in this manner: "You sound like a broken record!" That's because vinyl phonograph records had a habit of getting easily scratched or damaged if they were not handled with great care. A scratch or damage could cause the needle which picked up the sounds from the grooves in the recording to get stuck in one place, playing the same brief sounds over and over again until the needle was moved.

People who lack good communication skills tend to repeat their points over and over again. This is annoying and extremely unproductive. They sound like a broken record. However, there are times when you can use repetitive speech during a conversation or presentation to your advantage. If the person or group you're speaking to seems to be ignoring you during a critical point that you're trying to make, there is nothing wrong with coming back to it later in the form of a summary.

Whether you are having an open conversation with others involved or making a presentation, it's very important to stay focused and keep everyone else focused on what you are trying to communicate to them. Repetition is not the best way to do this. Instead, try these methods:

1. Maintain eye contact with your listeners.

2. Do not immediately respond to criticisms or questions designed to bait you into losing your train of thought or to move the discussion away from your message.

3. Be animated, but make sure you insert enough calm into your presentation or discussion to make certain that you do not appear to be a carbon copy of every other speaker they have heard a thousand times over. Do NOT use annoying cookie-cutter communication phrases like, "Let's put that on the back burner," or "Let's run that up the flag pole and see how it flutters." Avoid text message speak (generally, it makes people sound like idiots when they are not actually texting).

4. Follow through with each point you make, but do not over-state the obvious or provide more information than is needed for the moment.

5. Avoid making pronouncements of doom (listing all the bad things that will happen if they do not agree with your facts) and never make any part of your speech or conversation an ultimatum (they had better listen to you or else).

6. Do not preach, rant or lecture. If you sound like your third grade teacher, a fire and brimstone preacher or a motivational speaker at an insurance or real estate seminar, you are out of luck!

7. Offer sound advice in the form of suggestions, but never shovel it into the ears of your listeners.

8. Do not assign blame or overly criticize your audience. People quickly tune out negative speech. We have all heard people say, "I felt threatened by that presentation." If so, the presentation was a complete waste of time.

9. Keep any final summation short. Do not over-simplify your points, but do not over-state or drag them out by repeating your entire presentation of each either.

10. Have a short summary of your presentation available in print or ready to be emailed to any interested parties. Try to get as many of your listeners to accept your summary as possible. It will give them a chance to revisit your ideas at a more convenient time. Keep your summary short (one to two pages is preferable) with hot points and short explanations or definitions.

11. Know what you're talking about. Make sure that you have thoroughly researched your subject so that you will not be surprised or embarrassed by information that someone else may have that you do not know about.

Getting your point across is never just about saying words, it's about communicating feelings, back and forth, and having respect for your listeners and their viewpoints. Any important conversation or presentation should always make your listeners feel that you:

- respect differing opinions on the subject at hand without compromising your own.

- understand that the subject may cause people to express strong feelings about it and that you will not feel offended if they do.

- are willing to learn from others who may have another point of view as long as they are willing to learn from you as well.

- will listen to and consider the facts and views presented by everyone present without prejudice.

The key to successfully getting your point across is to:

- Use, not abuse, repetitive speech.

- Open doors instead of closing them.

- Keep your listeners engaged and interested and show them respect.

Make people want to hear your side of the story. You can do this by using some of the suggestions I have offered. It's all about looking at your audience as individuals, each with different personalities and perceptions of what you're saying to them.

Chapter Nineteen: Five Characteristics of Achievable Goals

Anyone with a desire to move ahead in their life in one way or another has made the decision to set personal goals. These goals should inspire self-confidence, hope and motivation. They should reflect a person's values, include their dreams and be able to be achieved in a series of well-planned out steps. There are five things that all truly achievable goals have in common...

1. Goals should be big enough to be challenging, but small enough to be realistic.

There is nothing wrong with dreaming big. Many great inventions and ideas came about because someone dreamed big. Big dreams, however, often require a series of small steps. It is impractical to believe that you can simply Will your dreams into reality. When you create a list of goals, do so with this in mind and think in terms of taking a series of small steps along a road that leads to your ultimate destination.

2. Goals should be specific.

You cannot plan out the ways and means to achieve a goal if it is merely a fuzzy idea that you may or may not have interest in by the time you finally decide to go for it. Many people are terrible procrastinators when it comes to decision making. Choosing specific goals helps us to overcome the desire to put off making important decisions. It also allows us the opportunity to achieve a dream that really means something to us. Decisiveness motivates, while indecision hesitates.

3. Goals should be realistic.

Having the desire to become a millionaire, quit drugs or find the perfect person to spend your life with are realistic and achievable goals for most people. Wanting those same things to happen overnight is unrealistic and doubtful. If you are thinking BIG when it comes to a goal, be sure you examine your ability to achieve that goal and allow for an honest time frame to do so. Short cuts tend to produce temporary results. I think that we all want results that will last when it comes to achieving our goals.

4. Goals should have a positive effect and outcome on your life.

Too many people are motivated by negative thoughts and actions. Revenge, for example, should not be part of a goal or the motivation for one. Positive motivation is always superior when it comes to goal setting. The desire and goal to earn more so that you and, perhaps, your family can live more comfortably is a better motivator than wanting to make more money than a friend, family member or even an enemy. Negativity sidetracks and can easily cause you to take dangerous or even illegal actions to achieve a goal.

5. Goals should be important enough to you to make you want to work towards them.

The primary reason that I encourage people to have specific and well thought-out goals is that they will probably have to work long and hard to achieve them. Goals should be the result of the passion you feel for something. Passion is a wonderful motivator that can easily keep you going through situations that may, sometimes, cause you to wonder if a goal you are trying to achieve is really worth the effort. Any goal you set should be important enough to you to be a life achievement that is essential to your confidence, motivation, passion and personal growth.

Epilogue

If you have any questions or comments, please feel free to email me at makelifeworkforyou@gmail.com

You can visit my web site at http://jsi4.tripod.com

Thank you for taking the time to read my book. Stop by my web site where i am constantly adding free articles and ebooks to help Make Life Work For You.

- Bill Edwards, 2012

www.ingramcontent.com/pod-product-compliance
Lightning Source LLC
Chambersburg PA
CBHW071544170526
45166CB00004B/1549